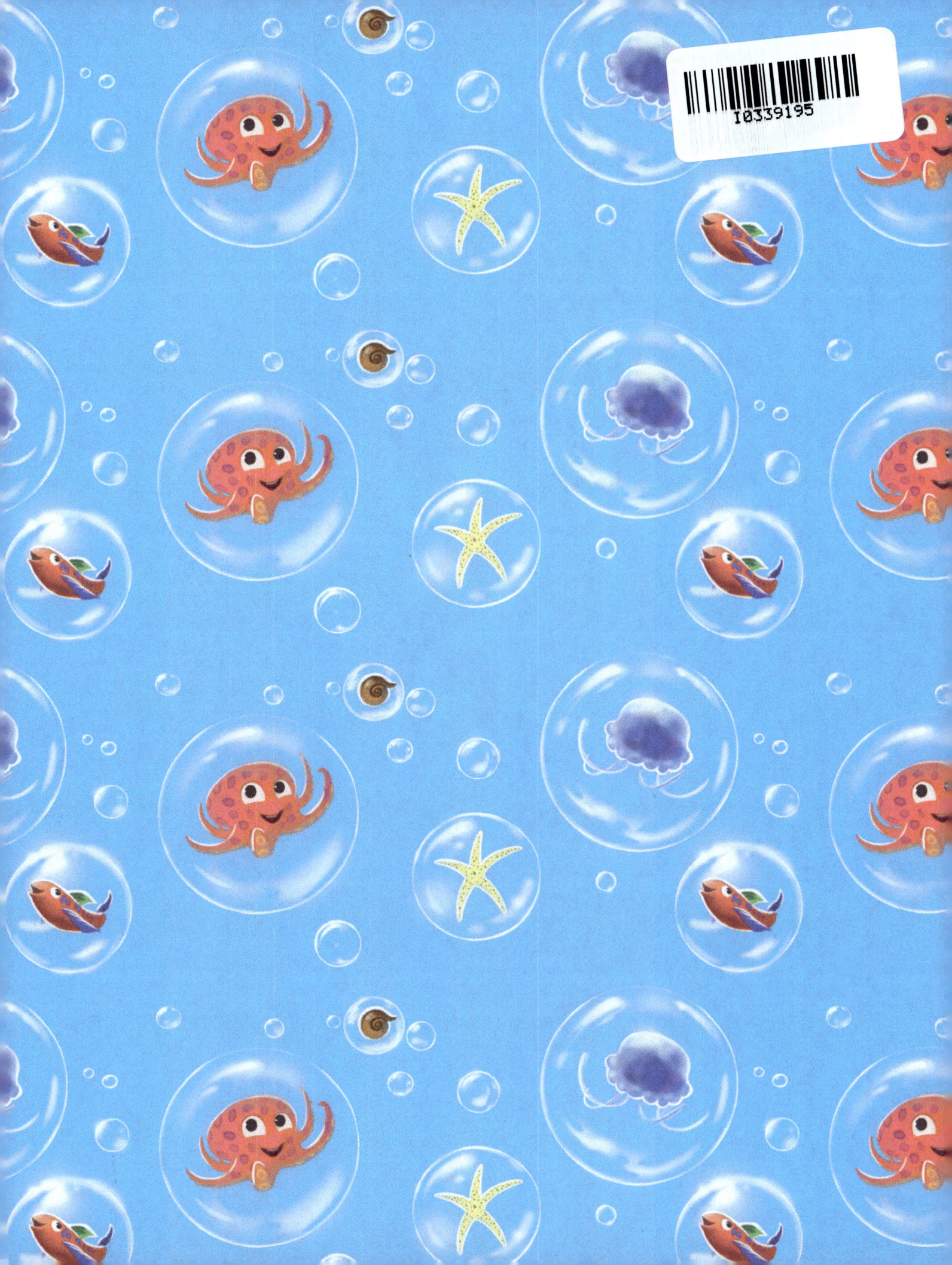

*To Amy, my gorgeous niece,
I hope you never stop dreaming!*

Text copyright © Chrissy Metge 2018
The moral rights of author and illustrator have been
asserted, this book is copyright.

Illustrations by Dmitry Chizhov

www.chrissymetge.com
www.ducklingpublishing.com

A catalogue record for this book is available from the
National Library of New Zealand.

ISBN - 978-0-4735-0356-7

Amy's Dreaming Adventures
The Underwater Paradise

By
Chrissy Metge

Amy loves fantasy, fairies and more,
But only in dreams can Amy explore.

So into her bed Amy jumps every night,
With Snowy her owl to help her take flight.

Almost as soon as she lays down her head,
Amy and Snowy fly far from her bed.
Off to a paradise they will soar.
Tonight in their dreams, a sea world's in store!

Now, Snowy has flippers that flappity-flop,
When he dives in the sea with a plippity-plop.

Her mermaid tail sparkles in the evening light,
As Amy leaps in joy at the night's delight.

Coral twinkles on the ocean floor.
 A brave seahorse comes to explore.
Soon more fish arrive to see
 Who this girl is, deep in their sea.

Darting out of the seaweed ferns,
 Cheeky fish do dances and turns.
They zip and dip and they dive through the weed.
 Amy giggles at their dizzying speed.

Then an octopus tells of a paradise lost
　　And a cave with a line that should never be crossed.

"A castle," it says, "that is big and bright,
　　has a guardian who patrols it all through the night."

The octopus points with legs galore,
"A very bright light is what you look for."

Amy swims on, then before her eyes...
"A light, with a cave underneath," she cries.

She swims up close, but the light is too bright.
"Who dares to enter?" booms a voice impolite.

"It's just me, Amy," she squeaks, soft as a mouse.
A shadow from beneath calls, "Who visits my house?"

She uncovers her eyes (behind hands she was peeping).
Shimmering in front is a creature leaping.

A magical merdragon glimmers in the sea,
    Near a glorious castle. "Have you come to see me?"

The Merdragon smiles. It's eyes open wide.
"I'm Meredith. Come and join me inside!

Do you like my cave, my home, my lair?"
Amy sees bubbles floating in there.

And high above her, bright twinkling lights,
Little creatures soar to amazing heights.

They swim with a twist and a turn and a razzle,
Wriggling and shining with a beautiful dazzle.

"They're my baby merdragons: one, two, three,
And they love blowing bubbles through the sea.

They will help you and Snowy return to the land.
Just let them show you and you'll understand."

The merdragons blow one bubble, then two.
They whisper, "One for Snowy and one for you.

Now swim inside and you'll float to the top.
It's like travelling inside a magic raindrop."

So into the bubbles Amy and Snowy go.
Watching the shimmering babies blow.

They rise to the surface then across to the land.
They float and bounce onto the sand.

Amy's mermaid tail bursts her bubble with a POP!

And onto the sand her feet land with a flop.
She bursts Snowy's bubble and out the owl flies.

"That was such fun!
 I wish we could do that again", Amy cries.

Amy knew it was time to go.
The time always comes,
whether fast, whether slow.

Back to her bed the travellers flew.
 Was it real? Just a dream? Amy knows. Do you?

THE END.

Chrissy Metge

With an extensive background and love of animation it seemed a natural progression to add childrens' author to her list of talents. As a new mother, one of her most favourite things is getting to see all the little things in life, all over again.

The Underwater Paradise is the second book in the series of Amy's Dreaming Adventures.